... a life in motion

(IN MOVEMENT THROUGH TIME)

By

Andrew Smith

DEDICATION

To the people, the places,

the paths crossed.

The journey, the voyage,

The time spent.

The beauty, the ugliness,

the victories, the losses,

the lessons, the learnings,

from gains and costs.

The loves, the losses,

the purpose, the meaning

the new sun, the rebirth

of a life lived.

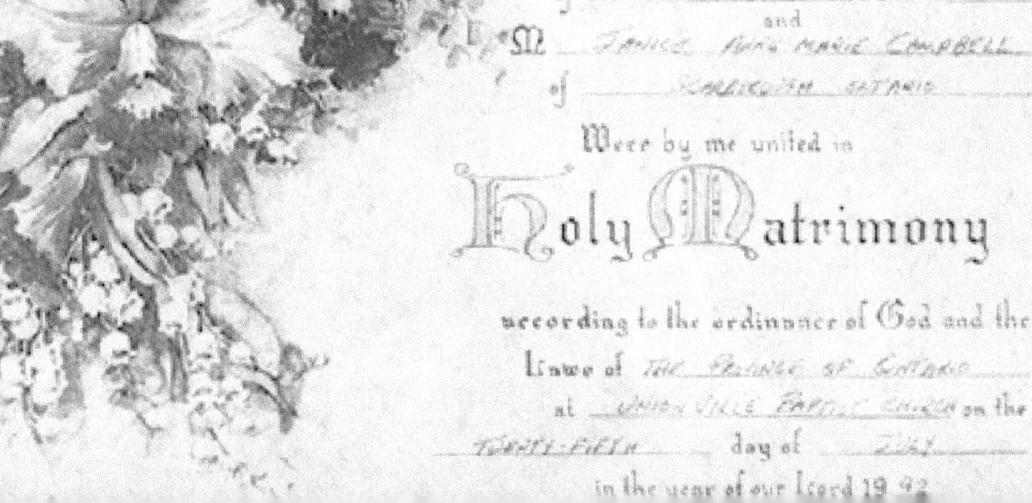

Mr. *Andrew Laine Fitzgerald Smith*

of *Scarborough Ontario*

and

Mrs. *Janice Ann Marie Campbell*

of *Scarborough Ontario*

Were by me united in

Holy Matrimony

according to the ordinance of God and the Laws of *The Province of Ontario* at *Unionville Baptist Church* on the *Twenty-Fifth* day of *July* in the year of our Lord 19 *92*

THE PRELUDE

Starting the day as before, catching you up on your life.

Uploading your memories, the moments, the sequence.

All of the gaps, in your time.

Confusion replaced the certainty; calm now, where once was noise.

Silence residing, evicting all sound,

Pandemonium now, in the past.

Speaking, mainly through actions; words no longer flowing with ease.

The lyrics now hard to remember,

Will become familiar with time.

We have always been connected; communicate on a higher level.

Words, awkward at times— they get in the way.

Blocking the feelings, the heart.

The sun now high in the sky shines its light, on our work.

Stick to the schedule, there is much to do.

No excuses, the time is now.

The answers are within our reach, though hidden, in plain sight.

Now, one day closer to the solution,

Our actions will lead us to the light.

CONTENTS

FOREWORD

Writing poetry is a cathartic experience. Through our poetry, we give ourselves permission to be unapologetically vulnerable with our deepest emotions. Our honest self-expression offers us a release—and maybe even the beginning of healing ourselves. Such vulnerability takes courage and authenticity. In Andrew's honest book of poems vulnerability is uniquely celebrated. It is a reminder to us all that we too have a story to tell.

I've mostly known Andrew Smith in professional settings. But I've always been aware of his love for lyrics, hip hop, and the arts during our meetings. Although I've been privy to some things in his life, after exploring this book of poems I see him in a new light both as a Husband and Father. As a young man, I'm inspired by his optimism and perspective in his poems.

When a poet finds their voice, the angels in heaven sing and the tectonic plates below our feet begin to rumble. Poetry is a universal language that allows us to have dialogue(s) normal conversations do not afford us. Our author, Andrew Smith, has found a voice of unconditional love, resilience, and joy. He uniquely navigates his experiences in a way that invites us, the reader, into life through his eyes.

Poetry is a bridge between the creative imagination and our unique human experiences. In A Life in Motion: In Movement Through Time, Andrew eloquently draws readers in with an uncanny seamlessness and care. Throughout the five chapters and forty-five poems, his rhymes schemes are playful, the cadence is effervescent, but the motions are visceral. He explores different ways of telling stories through a multitude of literary devices.

The poems are introspective and dance on a thread between subjectivity and objectivity. They invite us, the audience, to create our own meanings from Andrew's experiences. While these experiences may not be our own, there is a lot of meaning to gain that applies into our everyday lives.

Andrew's journey through love, family, and success intertwined with his plight of dealing with loss and adversity, and his metamorphosis through it all, is a mirror for us. Although our journeys may look different, the lessons, the perspective and the optimism to keep pushing through is something we can learn from. I often say that adversity doesn't discriminate—it doesn't care about who is good and who is evil—because it is inevitable. It's our response to adversity that ultimately brings us closer to our truth and purpose in life.

If you're looking for a happy ending, you've grabbed the wrong book. The happy ending is the whole journey. It is finding happiness through each experience in your life and the inspiration to keep pushing forward with a smile on your face.

Randell

Randell Adjei
Ontario's First Poet Laureate
Poet, Speaker, Author of I Am Not My Struggles

CHAPTER ONE

First Impressions

THIS IS WHY I AM WRITING

Purging.
Exploiting.
Leeching off my emotions.

Crying.
Bawling.
Keeping myself from falling.

Anger.
Pain.
On the cusp of insane.

Remember.
Forgive.
So many reasons to live.

Thinking.
Feeling.
Open to my healing.

Happiness.
Release.
Though the pain may never cease.

Acceptance.
At ease.
Finding my inner peace.

Spiritual.
Enlightening.
This is why I am writing.

MY WORLD

Do you see me?
You will hear me first, with the bass in my voice.
The rambunctious laugh, following a joke or comment unsuitable
for any situation.
This: the precursor.
Then my thick black-framed glasses, bright eyes, and welcoming
smile appear.

The door has now been opened.
You unknowingly and foolishly enter my world, the madness.
Where up is down, north is south, and east is west.
Where left is right, and right is ooh so wrong.
Where tears are replaced with laughter, yet we laugh 'till we
cry.

Where life stresses become the setup to a punchline.
Our interaction restores and reenergizes us.
We leave each other wanting more; thankful for the time
spent.

In this world, more is more and less is less.
There is an understanding that time is of the essence.
As time is a precious commodity that we can never ever
recoup.

In this world, we hear each other.
In this world, we see each other.
In this world, we understand each other.
In this world, we love each other.

MORE TO ME

There is more to me
Than you can see.

Beyond my skin, kissed by the sun.
No hair to pick, twist, braid, or curl.
A round, bald head, and fresh waxed shine.
My smile so bright, will make you blind.

There is more to me.
Than you can see.

Beyond the strut, that's in my step.
My confident, deliberate sway.
A friendly, easy-going nature.
To help you thwart your roughest day.

There is more to me.
Than you can see.

It has not always, been like this.
I've taken all that life has dished.
Rope-a-dope, wait for my time.
To strike and make the moment mine.

There is more to me.
Than you can see.

I am the iceberg, the unpeeled onion.
So much hidden, out of your sight.
The old broom, your tattered sweater.
Here with you; to win the fight!

This is the me.
That you will see.

But.

There is more...

I DO GETS HIGH

Not from rooms filled with smoke
Where drinks are shared with toasts.
All night; as we toke 'till we choke.

But, I do gets high.

Not from needles or heated spoons
That soothe life's painful wounds.
Strung out, as a lady sings the blues.

But, I do gets high.

Not from dancers that swear
They are only working for tuition.
And twerking is really not their ambition.

But, I do gets high.

Not from houses of ill repute.
With live fantasies that suit
Each and every possible desire.

But, I do gets high.

From...
Your smile.
Our Love and
Endless attraction.

Your touch;
Our desires; and
Constant interaction.

What we've shared.
How we've grown.
The life we've made.

The simple things;
That help pass the day.

Believe me.

I do gets high!

EMBRACING MY TRUTH

I try not to swear.
Profanity is beneath me.
Yet, so satisfying;
It refuses to leave me.

Vast riches of words;
In this language we use.
Yet none is so perfect;
To capture my mood.

I try to move on;
The past is the past.
At times it sneaks in,
To impact my future.

Second guessing and reliving,
The things I can't change.
An opportunity to use,
Profane words again.

My standard excuse?
"I did it; I tried!".
Sheltering behind,
My weakness; this lie.

No longer will I hide,
Behind my BIG lie.
Convincing myself,
That I really did try.
Embracing my truth,

Without an ounce of fear.
The sad realization;
I love to swear!

@#&$!

I LAY MY HEAD DOWN

I lay my head down.
I am tormented.
Tossing and turning.
Unable to escape. Nowhere to hide.

The choice I make is to succumb.
A flood of consciousness follows.
Topics, Ideas, concepts, feelings.
A portal has been opened.
My third eye awakened.

First,
I check:
Is this stream of knowledge contagious?
Has it been coupled with a wet dream?
No—not the one of our teenage days.
But the unfortunate accidents of our senior years.

I reach for my phone to scribe.
Words, sentences, and paragraphs follow.
Black letters on virtual white paper.
The process freeing.
I have found my North Star.

Fast flowing and overwhelming.
I go with this current, ride its wave.
Up and down the emotional scale.
It takes me where I need to go.

This, the result.
So much more than its parts.
Strength, weakness and feelings.
Patterns, rhythms and flows.

With this burden now released.
I am free.

I lay my head down.
I am at peace.

MY LOVE

My Love is...
Long.
Always growing.
Never too much.
Enough; & serves its purpose.

My Love is...
Hard.
Forged steel.
Solid as a rock.
A mass; immovable & unbreakable.

My Love is...
Lasting.
Over time.
Eager to work overtime.
On time; & works, on your time.

My Love is...
Forever.
An immortal soul.
Spanning many lifetimes.
Loyal; will find you next lifetime.

My Love is...
Never failing or premature.
Exactly what you are looking for.
Unrelenting & unashamed.
A constant; never-ending flame.

My Love is!

CHAPTER TWO

Unconventional Joy

ALONE

Through out my life, I have never been.
Alone.

From my family home,
I moved into your arms.
Just in our teenage years.
Most thought, "how cute."
Puppy love of the gullible youth.
They did not know we were BIG dogs.

Promising each other to never leave each other.
Alone.

Through higher education
We travelled our courses together.
Got married;
So in LOVE and committed.

We knew we would never leave each other.
Alone.

We worked through our professions.
Learning valuable lessons.
Passing on our knowledge.
To the babies we were raising.

What a life; we will never leave each other.
Alone.

Then, you broke your promise.
A stroke took your body.

For a week you were, non-responsive.
You liar!

Are you really leaving me?
Alone.

Thank God! You would wake.
Recover; recuperate
Now rehabilitating.
A hard lesson.
So much; not in our control.

A warning; one day we will leave each other.
Alone.

Our lives are temporary.
The promises we make;
Don't last forever.
But, until that inevitable day.

I promise; you will never be.
Alone.

LOST AND FOUND

You are here with me, by my side.
I feel your warmth,
Your love, your smile, and your touch,
In you I continue to see that which is familiar.

I feel a sense of comfort and joy as I watch you navigate
Your new world and your new mind, in your new body.
Yet these things you find new are not new at all.
They are merely a rediscovery of you from the past.

Your facial expressions when you are joyous, angry, confused, and sad.
The way you stroll, dance, and move.
Your dimples, that giggle, and gut belly laugh.
The joy you bring to all within your orbit.
You are there!

With time we continue to repair and rebuild your mind and your memories,
Our memories.
And with time, I see more and more signs of you. So many signs of you.
You are there!

You are here with me, by my side.
Lost yet found, by my side.

IF I WERE YOU

I want to know, just who you are.
The one who understands you.
To be to you that open door.
The first one that you reach for.

What if it was possible?
To change who we are today.
What would my views turn out to be?
Would they change, so radically?

If I were you, and you were me.

If through your eyes, I could see.
How would others react to me?
And my response, what would it be?
Would it be, so differently
From the me, that used to be?

If I were you, and you were me.

It turns out, I would be the same.
Even through this massive change.
We do not think so differently.

If I am you, and you are me.

In you, there is joy and pain.
You've been trained, by adversity.
Possess a love that is deep.
To match that of the great blue seas.

This is who, you are to me.
As.

I am you, and you are me.

SHORT SUPPLY

Your voice is a luxury to me.
As your words are now in short supply.
Never coming close to my perpetual demand for them, neither in volume or quantity.
It is strange to me.
As

There was a time, a time when...
The supply of this luxury was in abundance.
There was a time, a time when...
Unknowingly my demand for your voice and words suffered from this very shortage.
Please forgive my ignorance.
As

At that time, despite your diminutive stature, spaces were filled with your voice and your words.
Your words went over me, around me, through me as they comforted me.
Sadly, your words were not appreciated or reciprocated as they are today.

It was not so long ago, but it is so far away. If I only would have!
But life does not work like that. It provides the opportunities at the time.
Now, you are silent.

Silent but not quite.
Your eyes scream of a soul that has spent a lifetime working and caring for others.
They gleam and sparkle, as they always have, bellowing out unconditional love, joy, and innocence.

They also whisper the need for rest and recuperation.
This you shall have in abundance.

It is my wish to once again have all my spaces
filled with your voice and your words.
But today...
But today...
But today...

Your voice is a luxury to me.
As your words are now in short supply.

LIFE'S GIFT

With desire magnified
By what's been deprived.
And resolve strengthened.
Emotions put aside.

With a mind determined
To stay the full course.
And a strong, healthy body.
To sustain the harsh force.

With the strategy in place;
It's task in play.
The fruits of your labour
Will be realized, one day.

Your patience is wary.
Stretched to it's end.
Lean on me, beside you
When you need a friend.

Look where you are;
And from where you began.
The solution is clear.
Stick to the plan!

There is no hurry.
This race, not for the swift.
The journey is your reward;
And your life is the gift.

LIFE SENTENCE

This is truly an interesting fix.
One in which I cannot escape.
A by-product of time's control.
This sentence I serve, without parole.

A judges gavel gave me life.
A birthplace on this rock.
But these poignant and brilliant observations.
Come from this prisoner, of earth's nations.

As time would have it, I fell.
First in friendship, then in love.
A courtship through my youthful phase.
Resulting in my marriage days.

The judge's gavel struck two more times.
Over the years, as two boys arrived.
Both with similar fates to my own.
But this father was ready;
they'd never be alone.

Life's blessings and tragedies, I've experienced and accepted.
This paradoxical necessity of time.
It is the pains, that we will meet.
That make the victories, bitter;
yet sweet.

Judge again, strike the gavel in your court.
For all who will follow me.
Do as always has been done.
Offer life sentences; to everyone.

OUR NEST

At first it was you and me.
Life could not get any better; but it did.

We were invaded by these odd new creatures.
These creatures were needy, and strangely enough fulfilled our needs.
They were free—free to shit, pee, vomit, cry, and laugh whenever and
wherever.
We were kept very busy, taxiing them around to their many activities —
swimming, martial arts, music, and sports.
We would even take them on vacation with us.
Life could not get any better; but it did.

Our nest resonated with noise.
Crowded with toys, games, and the invaders' friends, who visited from time
to time and from near and far.
In the blink of an eye, one of the invaders' graduated from university and
moved out to his own nest.
The other invader left for college in a foreign land.
Our nest has now been emptied.
We are back to you and me.

Something has changed though.
These invaders are no longer needy; it seems like we have switched places
with them.
We know that they are GOOD and READY to explore and create their own
way. However.
We feel both needy and empty in their absence.
Yet filled with joy and pride with who they are, and who they will become.

Let it be written, known, heard, and proclaimed on this very day:
Our nest will always be here.
Here to welcome, guide, and protect these odd creatures it has nurtured
over the years.
Life could not get any better; but it will.

LIFE'S GARDEN

Its occupants grow,
And gain strength
Within its rich black soil.
The garden's devotion, unwavering.

It is their sanctuary.
Providing safety and protection,
Nurturing and nutrition,
To reach their full potential.

With the change in season
Comes the maturity of its occupants.
The garden's purpose now fulfilled.
They move on
Planting seeds in other gardens.

Our home, our garden
Now at the close of its season
Has served its purpose.

This sanctuary continues to exist
With its relevance continually growing.
Growing in magnitude with the passing of time
With its role continually diminishing.
Diminishing in magnitude with the passing of time.

This cycle plays out each generation.
It is the loop we are trapped in
And destined to complete.
It is our fate, the circle of life.

CHAPTER THREE

Unbalanced Forces

CHANGES

The bitter cold winter nights;
Amid the season's barren trees,
Iced earth; and frosted breath.
Keep me yearning;
Keep me burning,
For those long, hot summer days.
Waking me from, this winter daze.

The beauty of the autumn leaves,
They fall to earth, way too soon.
But not before revealing; palettes.
Brilliant kaleidoscopes of colour,
For all to witness, and be amazed.

The damp pungent spring air;
Soft and wet, muddy earth.
Rekindle the senses; usher in,
A new beginning, new seeds.
A new day; a new birth.
New, and renewed love.

The seasons guarantee change;
Its occupants have no immunity.
Changing as each season arrives;
Changing through their progression.

The difference is the point.
All serving a greater purpose.
Each puzzle piece is required;
To make the picture full; complete.

Change; it's impact will hit you.
For all your time here; in life.
The mistake is to ignore it.
Turn your back; refuse to face it.
The wise will closely hold it;
Willingly, and fully embrace it.

NEW YEAR MOVEMENTS

Spaceship earth, our birthplace, our home and our vehicle.
Remains in a constant state of motion.
We Are Moved!

Through day and night as we spin.
Through the seasons as we tilt towards and away from the sun.
Through the years each time our rotation around the sun gets completed.
We Are Moved!

Without our permission, choice or even consciousness.
We Are Moved!

As we approach the dawn of each new year.
We focus on an uncertain future and calm our nerves with broken promises
and straight-out lies;
New Year's Resolutions.

From now on, no more resolutions or promises to comfort this fool.
Only a commitment not to go through life simply being moved; but to move.

To move this body, this vessel that I inhabit with intention.
To move with purpose and consciousness
To do so in each moment in time.

And when I fail in a particular moment, commit to change and get back on
track the next moment.
...and not wait 'till the next time I; lap the sun.

THE WILDERNESS

I was born within it; in fact, we are all born within it.
The lucky ones, of which I count myself, do not know this fact.
We were coddled on arrival.
Protected from the wilderness by those responsible for our being, and those others who came before them.
Our beloved dead.

As we grow and become aware, there is an unfortunate reintroduction.
The wilderness seeps through the fragile and porous structures built by our loved ones to protect us.
Then at one point we become fully engulfed in the harshness of its reality.
At this time, we have a choice: collapse, stand still, or move.

At worst, our choices may result in our falling, crawling, and stumbling.
At best, our choices may result in our standing, walking, or even striding and running.
The results of our choices are not guaranteed and may not even be revealed in a logical order.
We must choose with care, not recklessly.
Choosing to move for movement's sake is not the way.
It increases the possibility of moving backwards instead of forward.
The wilderness can be cruel, unpleasant, and unforgiving.

Our choices do however assist in fulfilling its purpose
For us to learn, gain strength, and pass on its lessons.

To pass on its lessons to the lucky ones:
Those who are or will be coddled on arrival,
Those who's being you are responsible for,
Those who came and will come after you,
Those to whom you will become their
Beloved dead.

THIS ROAD

Unlevelled and unpaved
Built from the earth
You can see
The stones and the mud

With a foundation of pain
Strengthened by tears
Kept together
With shit and blood

And barely the room
For those who must
Venture and travel
Night or day

No lights, no signs
No maps, no markings
To assist
Along the way

We are on this road
But not by choice
None would select
This path

Fate's lottery
Commenced this journey
We unwillingly accepted
Its wrath

So hand in hand
And step by step
Careful and cautious
We move

Enjoying the view
And loving each other
We have nothing else
To prove

Its lessons we'll keep
And continue to carry
No matter where
We travel

Highway or bridge
Street or bypass
This road simply made
From gravel

This road though unlevelled
Will balance you
This road though unpaved
Will build you

This road

I WONDER

Wonder.
Ponder, the purpose.
The reasons and the meaning.
Of it all.

Wander.
At times, through time,
Losing time, purpose, and direction.
Lost in the madness.
Of it all.

Focus.
Strategize, make my plans.
Execute and measure the results
Of it all.

Question.
My choices, my tenure,
Our beginnings and end.
Does it matter? What's the point?
Of it all.

Continue.
With determination and resolve.
Faith and hope,
In the process and progress
Of it all.

Yet, throughout all my time,
This mantra loops through my mind:
I Wonder, I wonder, I wonder.

THE STORM

I don't hate anymore, not like I use to.
The anger left starved, with nothing to feed on.

The pain still remains, from the storm's devastation.
My tolerance now raised beyond what existed.

Not numb anymore, and deprived of sensation.
The coldness has faded; the warmth is returning.

I am able to feel, my range of emotions.
With capacity expanded, now I am open.

Taking the time to see-through the aftermath.
Clearing the way for a brand new path.

With obstacles removed, I know where to journey.
For the first time, facing my new reality.

The storm was intense, severe and extreme.
It's remnants to be carried for many years to come.

Like memories the storm's impact is sure to fade.
Yet my direction has forever been changed by the storm.

PAIN

Pain is our passport through life.

It is both friend and foe.
A dependable doubted companion.
Lingering around us.
Too close for comfort.

It is a constant vulnerability.
Just around the corner.
Looming in the background.
Lurking in the shadows.

Patiently waiting for its moment.
Pain will find its moment to
Strike!

Endure it; bear it?
Sometimes.
Feel it; buckled by it?
Sometimes.

Its acceptance will redefine you.
Open you up to growth.
Strengthen and fortify you.
Prepare you for the life ahead.

The alternative is to ignore it.
But the result?...

Well, the choice is yours
Always.

RAGES FIRE

Your rage matched only
By volcano fire
Is now extinguished
With a tsunami of tears

Then drowning in
A pool of your sorrows
Terrorized by the worst
Of all your fears

Re-enacting the steps
Of a time in the past
Stuck in a loop
That searches for blame

It's like

Travelling a road
With no destination
A futile effort
That will drive you insane

Try to awaken
From your deep slumber
Solutions will not
Be realized in dreams

A sober mind
A plan
Followed by action
Is your opportunity
To be redeemed

The choices are yours
Options exist
Each day until
You expire

But first

Pour out your tears
Fill up your pool
And extinguish all
Of rage's fire

CHAPTER FOUR

The Renewal

I GOT WORDS TOO

...yeah, I got words too.

All kinds of words.
Words for my inner and outer voice.
Words for the front of and behind closed doors.

Unyielding words that will make love to your ears and offer no protection.
Beat up on your ego without as much as a pause.

Different words for every room.
From the board room to the bedroom.
They can change your mood, and your emotions; your thoughts and your
actions.
My words can make and break your day.

...yeah, I got words too.

But I choose my words carefully.
It is my choice to use words that build. Leaving you:
Greater than;
Better than;
Stronger than;
More than before our interaction.

But, take care and approach me with respect and caution, 'cause

...yeah, I got words too!

LOSE MY TEMPER

No—I did not lose my temper.
I knew exactly where it was.

My blood was warm;
But not close to a boil.
My body, not tensed.
My fists, not clenched.

A voice:
Loud, deep, and rough
Required to make my point.
What seemed like screams
Were cluttered, thought streams.

No—I did not lose my temper.
I knew exactly where it was.

It started in my gut
With a deep sinking feeling
That cultivated, grew, and:
Travelled up and expanded

And freed itself, from my body
Flew through the air and
Greeted you; then exploded.
Of these facts, you are aware.

No—I did not lose my temper.
I knew exactly where it was.

SPECTATORS EULOGY

Your well placed seat
Gives you the best view
Your perspective is perfect
If only they knew

You see the forest
All of it's trees
The vast green woodland
Everything in between

You have the right
To second guess these fools
To straight out criticize
They don't have your eyes

Their missed opportunities
Their substandard decisions
You'd have done better
They need your vision

They proceed to play out
Their unsound ways
You get to witness
Their errs each day

The last laugh is yours
You've made no mistakes
Made no decisions
That impact your fate

Smile as your wooden box
Descends below the earth
One to six feet
This
Your final seat

You've been a spectator
Fearful to make mistakes
This role consumed your time
Now it's too late

NEEDS

You don't know what you need.
When you are in need of your wants.

Wants controlled by what you've seen.
A tragic scene; it will end badly.

Trying badly to impress your peers.
They only peer into the life that you show.

You show the things that you collect.
What you collect leaves you empty.

Empty your space, you need the room.
The room, unoccupied just like you.

Can you continue in this game?
A game playing you without an ending.

Ending this cycle, your main task.
A task to discover all of your needs.

Needs are all the simple things.
The simple things that give you life.

A life of peace, hope and love.
Love will fill, the space in your heart.

A heart filled with love is giving and open.
Open to all the things that you need.

THE MASK

Without cover or protection.
Acting or posing.
You wake, to start the new day.

Unrestrained.

Before you don your mask of deceit.
You are comfortable and at-ease.
Without walls or barriers.

Genuine.

Not a victim of pride.
Not exaggerating your strengths.
Or concealing your weaknesses.

Exposed.

The show has not begun.
But the curtains will open soon.
Don't do as you do every other day.

Forget about the mask you wear.
It's false image, determined to project,
and reflect a you that is not

You.

Maybe today is the day.
The day to eliminate all pretenses.
Suspend make-believe and reconcile
the inward and outward you.

Truth.

Put your fears aside and trust in me.
Let me decide if I like what I see.

It is now time to reveal all.

That which is unrestrained.
That which is genuine.
That which is exposed.
That which is you.

The truth.

TIME

Its speed varies
There is a correlation
Between it
And our respect
Of it

It is our past
We live in it
Savouring our foundation

It is our future
We anticipate it
Looking forward to its arrival

it is our present
We overlook it
Without acknowledgement

It moves in extremes
At a snails pace
In the blink of an eye
Stops

In reality
It is our perspective that's flawed
Time is not the variable
Our attitudes blind us

Time's pace is constant

During a hot summer day
On a long weekend
A Friday afternoon at work
Or spending time with loved ones

It moves in one direction
Forward not backwards
Not stopping
Never resting

Time takes no time for time

YOUR DREAMS

You close your eyes and sleep
Under my watchful eyes.
Your chance to rest and recoup
And reconstruct your mind.

The past, present, and future
All places near and far.
Existing in the here and now
Made possible in your dreams.

Where will you be carried?
At what point in your timeline?
Be you my devoted wife or girlfriend?
My sweet thing or a stranger?

Am I your hero or a villan?
A friend or your foe?
Dressed to the nines or casual?
In a trench coat and speedos?

Not my choice or decision.
Your dreams belong to you.
Just know if you're disappointed
It's 'cause I'm wearing speedos in the damn cold!

IN RETROSPECT

It was a little unfair of me—
Dare I say, somewhat selfish—
Placing you in this thankless role.

Protecting me from me?

Cleaning up my word soup
Right in the middle of the flow.
You were fully employed;
Albeit, working overtime.

It usually started with your stern look,
The rolling of your eyes,
The kissing of teeth, successively.

Then clueless Me: ignoring all dat!
And you cleaning up the mess.
Putting me back on track.

Oh, how I miss it all!

The silent treatment.
The long tense ride home.
My empty promises, never to repeat the scenario.
The making up.... well let me not say too much.

Now I roam, with the potential to BE
Unlimited, unfiltered.
Unrestrained and unprotected.
Messy and dare I say, a little dirty.

Everything I always wanted!
But nothing I ever needed.

Hindsight is really twenty twenty.
No truer words spoken.

As in retrospect,
The thrill exists BECAUSE there are limitations.

MY MISSION

I aim to BE that which I profess:
The manifestation of my ideals.
Carrying the burdens of my imperfections.
Which is only human;
The league that I belong to.

Rooted in the ancestry of a mother.
A land with origins in science, wisdom, and understanding.
Rich in resources and in culture;
With drum and bass setting the pace.

Transplanted now to a new land.
Sowing my seeds in time for the harvest.
A husband, a father, a family man.
All this possible, following a plan.

A man, a gender.
I choose not to ignore.
Yet another flaw to overcome.
Balancing my ego with my abilities.
Recognizing when to lead and when to follow.

On this earth to seek and learn.
Not swaying from this humble position.
Staying focused; fixing my vision.
Advancing my ideals, towards my mission.

AS WE SHARE THIS SPACE

I think of the chances.
The choices we've made.

And the role of fate...
Is this out of our hands?
Do we have control
Over the places we land?
Or just along for the ride?

Look where we've been...
Having travelled so far.
From different locations.
Now to be where we are.

Spending our time...
The need to be stingy.
This sacred commodity.
Spending it wisely.

Deep understanding...
Finding myself.
By getting to know you.
Seeing me through you.
Enhancing inner vision.

Community...
For what is the purpose
Living only for me?
For a life that is empty
And void of real meaning.

Harmony...
As we share this space.
Together for life.

CHAPTER FIVE

The Lessons

I CANNOT KEEP A SECRET

I cannot keep a secret
And keep it in my mind.
It must be released
Before the end of my time.

Be careful of your choices;
All of your actions.
The way you move,
The things you say.

I'll reveal it.
In my writings,
Be you friend or foe.
Use it against you
When I hold my court.

You see, I am the judge,
The jury and executioner.
The one who makes the laws
That will convict you.

So I WILL tell on you
Without a second thought.
My word is my bond;
Have no doubts.

I do offer you a bargain,
Not in the form of a plea.
That my court will always be fair,
Because I also Tell on ME.

THE CONDITION: LIFE

The good news
This condition
From which I suffer
Is temporary

And I am not alone
Astonishingly enough
Those who suffer from it
Said to be in the billions

The bad news
This condition
From which I suffer
Is temporary

Though the sufferers are many
Said to be in the billions
Astonishingly enough
Its conclusion is faced alone

Life by definition
A temporary state of being
As is
All that exists within it

Use each moment

As if
As if
Your life depends on it
Because
Because
It really does

LAB RAT

Uncertainty, the driving force.
Compelling you to make a change.
The path you take will set the stage.
And move you on to you're next phase.

You see, it's all simply just a test.
A laboratory, where you're the rat.
You've run the maze and found the cheese;
Are unfulfilled and not at ease.

Breaking this cycle, you jump the wall;
Prepared for the drop and discomfort.
To the peanut gallery, you're just a fool.
This process required, to refine your tools.

With no regrets, now on your way
To soar like a bird, or fall to the earth.
An exciting time, to make your own choice.
An opportunity, to express your true voice.

Building a life that is truly your own.
Void of the outside voices of destruction.
Avoiding the war and finding the peace.
Finally living a life of ease.

A SELFISH LIFE

Your focus on cost
Costs you more in the end.

Always wanting something
At someone else's pain.

A something for nothing
Type of hue, man!
Will never brighten your colour
Or shine your light.

Blind to the benefit,
To you and to yours.
Living selfishly;
Just for you.

Taking from others;
Emptying their cupboards.
Stealing their food,
And playing the victim.

Your endless greed
Consumes your character.
Now empty of principles,
You've stolen from yourself.

You stand before me
A soulless shell.
Overflowing with gluttony,
Sadness, and sloth.

With anger and pride
Guiding your way.

This, your cost,
You MUST bear it!
Now where is the benefit,
That drove you here?

You selected this life style.
The way you chose to BE.

But is this the way?
To live and never see?

FREEDOM

It is a relative concept,
This thing called freedom.
To be unhindered and unrestrained.
Ironic though, to be under the reign
Of those "reclaiming" their freedom?

It seems that this freedom,
As unlimited as it proposes to be,
Is limited in its distribution.
To whom; to who?
When and where?
To you and not me?

A dangerous concept though,
To the undeveloped mind.
The children and the child minded.
The breastfed and the coddled.
The umbilical cord attached:
Snowflakes.
The "patriot"?!
Melting in the anger of their own discomfort.

Oh, their beautiful proud fantasies of:
What use to be;
What still should be;
What is going to be; and
What must be!

Stuck in an endless loop—
Trapped in the hell of—
Their alternative reality.

Not what freedom is to be.
Not what freedom is to me.

LIMITATIONS

Me,
Spending time convincing you
Of what you won't see.
You can't see; your vision is limited.
Blinded by the constraints you place on you.

It's like peeing into the wind, and expecting not to get wet and stink.

I:
The subject, not the victim,
Of a marketing campaign with no control over the narrative.
Your position reflects the errors in your consumption.

Common sense never impacting your arguments.
Limited.
The beat and rhythm not a consideration during your dance.
Strange.

Odd—
As our presence provides opportunities for growth.
If we remain exactly the same as we were in years past, time has been wasted
Spent frivolously, without purpose or direction.

We
Are never just a caricature;
A simple reflection of a narrative.
The mirror is not real.
It is merely a figment of imagination.

Contrary to popular belief,
Breaking the mirror is the solution.

The fate of bad luck is a lie.
Opportunities will open up.

Open up other ways of BEING.
Without past limitations.

TOLERANCE

Tolerance

It suggests but never promises
Implies but never delivers

Acceptance

We tolerate that which we despise
The things we must bear
For the sake of

We embrace that which we accept
And endure that which we tolerate
Enthusiastic affection
Versus
Irritation and suffering

On the surface
And in practice
They appear identical
But they differ to the core

Relationships

When founded on tolerance
They are built on shaky ground
Limited in depth
Fragile
Subject to
Untrustworthy whims

And ultimately destined to fail

Acceptance is infinite
Impervious to
The unreliable winds of change

Different sides of the same coin

Time

The great arbitrator
Determines and reveals
Which side of this coin
We land on

THE MINER

Beneath the surface,
It's where I dig.
Through my discomfort,
To where my soul lives.

Here lies the truth,
Where I now reside.
Beyond the physical,
Emotions put aside.

In this location,
There is no fear.
No outside burdens,
That I must bear.

A strong foundation,
Honest and pure.
I build my future,
Safe and secure.

The words that live,
In this space.

Will move your body,
And free your mind.

Touch your soul;
Recharge your heart.

Change its beat,
Make anew, a restart

Molest your thoughts,
Question your ways.

Change your actions,
For all your days.

Hear: lie the words,
For the right situations.
Be you of clear mind,
And use careful consideration.

I REMEMBER THE TIME BEFORE

I remember, the time before...
Life lasted forever.
The pace was so fast.
The tasks were too many;
We chased our tails,
In hopes of its capture.

I remember, the time before...
From friendship to love.
The foundation of marriage.
The birth of three babies.
Boy, girl, boy.
Jelani, Jamoke, Jabari.
Two of which would live,
Who turned to boys.
Then claimed their manhood.

I remember, the time before...
A victim of time.
Not in our control.
Too little spent together.
Together; a scarce luxury.
The We; divided and conquered.

I remember, the time before...
The promise to slow down.
After this or after that.
Once this is achieved
We can finally do those things,
The things we LOVE together.

This: the time before...
Before your stroke.
Before your coma.
Before the hospitals;
Their machines and tubes.
Before the reality
Of OUR mortality.
Before your near death.

Now in the present...
You are reborn.
Life has its limits.
The pace not so fast.
Not so many tasks.
Though daunting, yet attainable,
We chase our health,
In hopes of its capture.

This is the time...
Now!

A LIFE IN MOTION

I live a life unstill.
Moving even as I stand.
Still.

Well rested; not restless.
In motion, yet to the naked eye,
Still.

Vibrating from the inside, only to expel.
Catching the vibes reciprocated.
For my soul's purpose, to excel.
Still.

Never pristine or perfect,
Though this is my will.
Always learning and growing.
Yet in appearance, I BE
Still.

What I have seen, I can't unsee.
What I have heard, I can't unhear.
Where I have been, I can't un-BE.
All of which has created this: ME.

For this I am grateful
Still.

Would not change a moment
Still.

For the ME, I would BE
Would not BE, ME.

Perhaps someone tormented
A tortured soul, filled with pain.
Having nothing to offer, but to BE
Still.

In ME there is thoughtfulness,
Deep consideration.
Plans put to action,
Despite much consternation.

Your mind is your canvas;
Paint me as you will.
I'll continue my life in motion,
As I appear to you as
Still.

WHO AM I?

A poet I am not
That title won't fit
Perhaps what I am
Is simply a snitch

Telling on life
Reporting its crimes
Occasionally putting
My tales to a rhyme

A joker
No
Though I do love to laugh
It is therapy
To remove the pain

But with this title comes
A burden too high
Leaving its victim
Alone on stage

A lover
Can't deny
I am legendary
This is how it plays out
In my mind

If this aint the truth
Not my reality
Thanks but no thanks
I'll stick to my fantasy
So who am I
In this deadly game
This game of life
That ends one way

I've been every title
That you can muster
The most important
Is who I will be

I am forever evolving
In a state of change

Working each day
To work it out

Never tiring
Always toiling

Till the day I rest
And figure it out

THE MAN THAT YOU NEED

You've been with me
Since I can remember.
Always there, right by my side.

Your body.
Your spirit.
Your mind.
Your soul.
All together, holding me high.

Be I young and black
Or old and grey.
All the contradictions of my days.

The energized optimist,
Or weary pessimist.
You always lead me
In the right way.

So you have fallen; can't get up.
Not strong enough on your own.
But we are joined, intertwined.
Together as ONE.

Our struggles
Test what we do;
To determine who we are;
Who we will BE;
When this life is done.

Life has left you, tired and weary.
Unbalanced, with blurred vision.
Difficult for you to see.

But I am energetic and optimistic,
Strong and proud.
I AM
The man that you need me to BE.

ACKNOWLEDGEMENT

Out of all the opportunities that I have been afforded in life, being an author was not even in the realm of my possibilities.

From this I've learned.

Life always has more for you.

When you experience more, more will come to you.

When you experience losses there is something more just ahead.

Be prepared to be unprepared, then simply go with it; your resistance is futile.

What is to be will be.

Surround yourself with people and spaces that grow you, feed you and love you.

It is these lessons that created this work.

Truly live your life in motion...in movement through time.

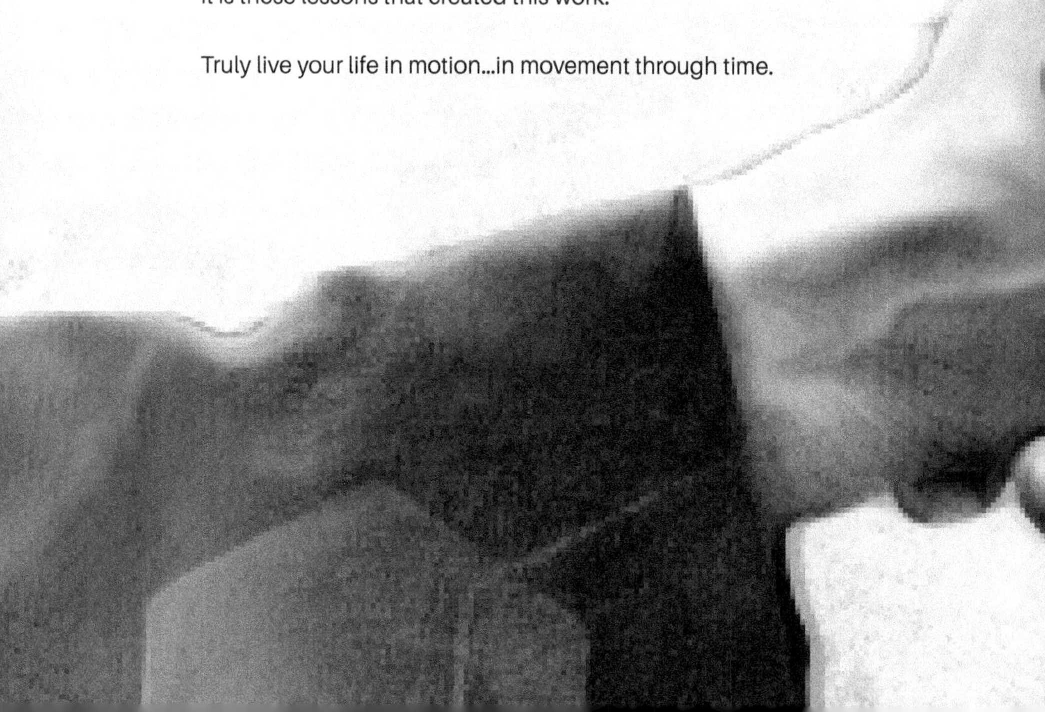